How to Lead an
Effective
Meeting

(and get the results you want)

Dick Massimilian

Richard D Massimilian
25 Highland Park Village #516
Dallas TX 75205

Ordering Information:
Orders by U.S. trade bookstores and wholesalers, contact the publisher above. Quantity sales. Special discounts are available on quantity purchases by corporations, associations, and others. For details, contact the publisher above.

Printed in the United States of America

Publisher's Cataloging-in-Publication data
Massimilian, Dick.
How to Lead an Effective Meeting (and get the results you want) / Dick Massimilian.
p. cm.
ISBN 978-0-9976222-0-1 (hardcover), ISBN 978-0-9976222-1-8 (paperback),
ISBN 978-0-9976222-2-5 (ebook)
1. Business 2. Adult Education

This book is for my wife,

Jeri Fritz.

The best day of my life, so far,

was the day I met her.

Table of Contents

Forward

Who is this Guy, and Why is He Writing this Book?

It seems these days that everyone hates meetings. How many times have you heard someone say, "We have too many meetings," or "I am booked so solid every day in meetings I never have time to get anything done," or "I'm back-to-back…"

But when you talk to people, it isn't that they hate meetings; it's that they don't like meetings in which nothing gets done. No one is sure why the meeting was called, or why half the people are in the room, or what exactly is supposed to get done, or what was decided. We complain about meetings, but we seem to attend more and more of them.

This book is for people who need to lead effective meetings, in any context. It is a blueprint for how to have your meetings work, defined as, meetings that achieve the results you want to achieve, in the meeting and afterwards. It's a how-to guide for using the time you spend planning, organizing and conducting meetings wisely. It's about getting results through meetings.

I have spent several decades as a management consultant and advisor to leaders. I have attended several thousand meetings and presentations. I have organized, designed, facilitated and led meetings for very small to very large groups, in the Americas, Europe, Asia and the Middle East. Those groups have included hourly workers, C-suite executives, parent volunteers, Boards of Directors, teenagers, senior teams, salespeople, professional service firm partners, and prison inmates. I have made every mistake that you could possibly make with regard to meetings. My hope here is that you avoid making at least some of those mistakes.

But my motivation isn't entirely altruistic. I too hate ineffective meetings. They waste time, energy and resources. I want to minimize the time I spend in those gatherings to the extent possible. I am on a mission to make meetings work.

Why are effective meetings important?

Meeting quality matters. Well-run organizations have well-run meetings. Sloppily run organizations have sloppily run meetings. What are the signs of a bad meeting? The meeting starts late. There is no agenda. The meeting runs over. No one is sure what if anything was decided or accomplished. The same meeting to discuss the same topic seems to be held over and over again. No one knows what the next steps are or who is supposed to follow up whom for what. Someone monopolizes the meeting and someone else talks in circles, while yet someone else seems to simply rephrase and repeat what has already been said.

Nothing discourages people, whether volunteers or employees, like feeling they are wasting their time. Too many meetings waste time. They sap morale, and leave people frustrated or irritated. This is a shame, as leading an effective meeting is not rocket science once you have a blueprint.

If, like me, you have an allergic reaction to wasting time in meetings, this book is for you.

It is divided into five principal sections:
- Preparation
- Invitation
- Agenda
- Delivery
- Follow Up

The sections outline the five phases of a meeting. For your meeting to be successful (again, defined as, a meeting that achieves the results you want to achieve), you must execute each phase successfully.

Meetings versus Presentations

The tips in this book are intended to apply to both meetings, in which various people interact in a more-or-less informal setting, and presentations, occasions on which a speaker presents material to an audience in a structured, more-or-less formal setting. Some principles apply more directly to meetings, others to presentations. All are relevant to both.

Part 1

Preparation: Putting the Rabbit in the Hat

As a wise woman once said, anyone can pull a rabbit out of a hat. But not everyone can put a rabbit into a hat.

That holds true for leading great meetings. The meeting itself is the easy (or, at least, the easier) part. The hard part is preparing for the meeting.

First things first: Purpose and Intended Results

To lead an effective meeting, you must be crystal clear about what you want to achieve. No one will understand your objectives unless you do. You have to demand ruthless clarity. The person with whom you have to be ruthless is yourself.

Write down the purpose of the meeting. Look at what you have written. Is that what you want to accomplish?

Then ask yourself, how will you know that you did that? These are your intended results.

Sometimes the intended result is inherent in the purpose. For instance, if the purpose of your meeting is to:

• Review the proposals submitted by three caterers and select a caterer for the reception, then your intended result is implicit. If at the end of your meeting you have selected a caterer, you have achieved the purpose of your meeting.

If, however, the purpose of your meeting is to:

• Plan the New Students Reception

Watch out. What exactly do you want to achieve in the meeting? Brainstorming a potential location and themes? Or do you want to select a location and theme? Do you want to leave the meeting with ideas for a menu? Or do you want to select a menu? Do you want to simply hear ideas, or do you want action?

If your preference is action, you might couple your meeting purpose of "Plan the New Students Reception" with some or all of these Intended Results:

• Identify a venue
• Select a theme
• Select the menu
• Pick a caterer
• Establish how we will invite people and when

Clarity and specificity are key here. We may think we know what we want, but when asked to state what we want, we may find we can't readily do that. Alternatively, we may have a clear idea of what we want to achieve, but no one else will unless we state our objectives succinctly and specifically. Here, written repetition helps a lot.

Draft your initial statement of the purpose of your meeting. Put aside what you have written, go off and do something unrelated, come back in a few hours or the next day and reread what you have written. When I do this, I am often surprised, because what I thought was very clear actually isn't when I reread it. You will likely see ways to sharpen or clarify what you actually intend when you focus on what you want to achieve. Multiple iterations are not only likely; they are desirable.

Don't be in a rush to articulate your purpose. Slow down now so that you can speed up later. The meeting purpose is like the trajectory of a rocket. If you want a rocket to land on the moon, it is best to be precise about calibrating its direction. It is not a good idea to aim the rocket for outer space and hope for the best. The same holds true for your meeting purpose. Arguably the best way to make sure a meeting fails is to have a vague meeting purpose or worse, no meeting purpose.

In a Corporate Context

As a general rule, the larger the corporation, the more meetings held. This can be a plus, if the meetings are well organized and effectively led. But often, meetings are held out of habit rather than to produce action.

Why hold a meeting?

The best reason to hold a meeting is to produce **action,** often in the form of a decision that is actionable. The worst reason to hold a meeting is to share information. In the Internet age, there are countless ways to share information that are more efficient than compelling people to assemble.

In-person meetings to **build relationships** and establish a sense of camaraderie can be very effective provided that that meeting purpose is explicit. Granted, people can get to know one another via telephone, Skype and videoconference, but there is no substitute for face-to-face interaction to establish the bonds that characterize high performing teams.

Meeting can also be held to establish **alignment** among attendees, again, if that purpose is made explicit. Alignment is often an interim step needed to produce effective action. When the purpose of a meeting is to produce alignment among attendees, there are two essential prerequisites:

- Ensuring everyone who needs to align is present
- Ensuring everyone signifies his or her alignment via some physical act, such as standing or raising a hand

For example, let's say you work in a company that has a Sales Division with six Regions – each with a Regional Vice President (VP). You are the head of Human Resources (HR). You have drafted a revised sales incentive plan for next year and want the alignment of the six Regional VPs before announcing the plan. The plan is your decision, but as a practical matter you want and need their alignment with it.

You convene a meeting, stating the purpose of your meeting as *"to review the new sales incentive plan so that the Regional VPs understand, align on and endorse the new plan prior to scheduled plan announcement."* The meeting purpose is clear. The intended result is alignment, which you intend to make explicit at the appropriate time during the meeting. You work the calendar and find a date and time at which all six regional VPs can attend – a feat in and of itself – either in person or via telephone. You confirm the attendance of all six Regional VPs, and send the proposed sales incentive plan to them in advance so that they can each review it before the meeting.

Two days before the meeting, you get an email from the Northeast Regional VP, saying that she now must visit with a customer at the meeting time and therefore cannot attend.

You now have a dilemma. You need alignment of all six VPs, and you know from experience that unless they are together, you can't achieve the result you need. You consider your options. You could:

- Reschedule the meeting. But time is of the essence, and finding an open date that works for six busy people is a major challenge. Moreover, you are under a deadline to announce the new plan, so this option is not viable.
- Hold the meeting without the Northeast Regional VP. You could say, "five out of six is better than nothing." But then you don't have alignment of the Regional VPs, which is the point of the meeting.
- Call the Northeast Regional VP in advance, review the proposal with her, ask for her approval, obtain it, and announce her alignment at the start of the meeting. You have tried this in the past, and while in theory this could work, you know that in practice it almost invariably does not. The point of an alignment meeting is for everyone in attendance to talk through a proposal and reach a common understanding. If that isn't necessary, then there is no need for a meeting in the first place; simply have everyone sign off via email. So this too is not a realistic option.

What then should you do?

Refer back to your meeting purpose: *"to review the new sales incentive plan so that the Regional VPs, understand, align on and endorse the new plan prior to its scheduled plan announcement."*

You should visit with the Northeast Regional VP in person or, at a minimum, via telephone. Do not email her; it will not work. When you and she connect, you should say:

- *"Thanks for letting me know about the meeting. Understand. No problem. I'd reschedule if I could, but you know how tough the calendars are and we have to roll out the new plan soon. How would you like to weigh in on the plan? Would you like to designate someone to attend to act on your behalf? Just let the other Regional VPs handle it? I want to make sure you're included, since we will be moving ahead after the meeting and everyone's input is important. What works for you?"*

What's the message here? There are several:

- Your not attending is not a problem.

- And, at the same time, we are moving ahead. We can't wait for you.
- It's your call if, when and how you weigh in here.
- But this is "speak now, or forever hold your peace." After this meeting, the plan will be set.
- What do you want to do?

A conversation such as this is the only way you can achieve your meeting objective. If you avoid this discussion, postpone it until after the meeting, or pretend you can somehow bring the Northeast VP on board later, your chances of achieving your ultimate objective – endorsement of the plan so that the plan can be rolled out – are minimal at best.

There is a litmus test for alignment. If after a group aligns, all debate stops, alignment has occurred. If there is any second-guessing, further debate, or attempts to appeal or undermine, then something other than alignment has occurred. Alignment is more than everyone paying lip service in a meeting. It must be genuine and, for all intents and purposes, permanent. Unfortunately, often what people call "alignment" is anything but.

Beware of meetings without a stated purpose

Never call or lead a meeting without a clearly stated purpose. For that matter, if you are invited to a meeting, don't know the purpose and go without asking the meeting purpose at the start, it is your own fault. A sure-fire way to waste your own and other people's time is to sit in a meeting unsure of either why you are there or what the meeting is supposed to accomplish. If you don't know, ask. It's likely that you aren't the only one who doesn't know.

You've articulated your meeting purpose and are now ready to invite the people who should attend. The next questions is, whom to invite?

Whom to Invite?

The meeting purpose tells you whom to invite to the meeting. Start by asking, "What is the minimum number of people I need in the room to achieve what I want to achieve? Who *must* be there?" This is a different question from "Who will want to be there or who thinks she should be there?". You may well want to add those people later. But first things first: who has to attend?

Sometimes at this juncture, you may realize that for whatever reason, you cannot assemble the people you need to achieve the purpose of your meeting. If this happens, you have two options. You can change the purpose of the meeting. Perhaps your objective was too ambitious. Maybe you can achieve an interim step to your goal rather than your ultimate objective.

Your second option is to not have the meeting. You may not be ready. Perhaps you need to lay more groundwork, enroll more people in your plans one-on-one, or do further research. You are far better off waiting until you can be effective than you are convening a meeting prematurely.

In any event, look to your meeting purpose to determine whom to invite. Make sure you invite all the pigs, then see whether you have room for the chickens.

Pigs and Chickens

In bacon and eggs, the pig is committed; the chicken is involved. The pig is all-in. The chicken is not.

In an organizational context, the pig is accountable. The chickens are everyone else. You know you are the pig if, should the endeavor go wrong, you are the person who gets the phone call about it. Being a pig is almost always a solitary pursuit. Shared accountability is a great theory that rarely works in practice.

In bacon and eggs, the pig is not better than the chicken. You can't eat breakfast if one of the two is missing. You need both. The problem arises when you confuse pigs and chickens. This is especially true with regard to meetings.

Most meetings are comprised of both pigs and chickens. For example, consider a scenario in which the Head of Marketing – let's call her Claire – calls a meeting to design a new marketing campaign. She is the person ultimately accountable for the campaign's success; if the campaign is judged ineffective, her phone will ring. Here, Claire is the pig. She will decide what the campaign includes and what it looks like.

Claire invites her team to the meeting. She has four direct reports, all of whom have given her important input she will use in making her decision. These are chickens, but important chickens. Two of her subordinates ask if they can bring their summer interns with them to the meeting as a learning experience. Claire agrees. The interns are also chickens, but unimportant ones.

Knowing that the salespeople are very interested in the marketing campaign and have been critical of past campaigns, Claire now faces a dilemma. Bob, the Head of Sales, has been a past, vocal critic of marketing initiatives. Bob is a chicken, but a potentially disruptive chicken. On one hand, if Claire does not invite Bob to the meeting, she knows he is likely to feel that he had no input into campaign design and will be more likely to criticize it. On the other hand, Claire knows from past experience that Bob believes that as a function of his role, marketing campaigns must at a minimum meet with his approval. Bob thinks he gets to decide, when in fact he doesn't. He is a chicken who thinks he is a pig.

Claire and Bob have a cordial relationship as colleagues. Their relationship isn't marked by animosity, but also isn't particularly close. They are professional acquaintances. Claire wants Bob's support, but recognizes that his expertise is sales, not marketing. She values his input, but realizes she is ultimately accountable for the campaign, not Bob.

What should Claire do?

To maximize the chances of the success of both her upcoming meeting and her marketing campaign, Claire should:

- Invite Bob. He is a stakeholder in the marketing campaign. He has demonstrated past interest. He is likely to have valuable insight because he knows customers. He will appreciate the invitation. If he declines the invitation, Claire has at least invited him.

- Articulate the purpose of the meeting carefully, and in her invitation to Bob, state the purpose clearly. An effective statement of purpose would likely read something like:

    o "Solicit input from key stakeholders to inform the design of the marketing campaign." She could add, "Intended Result: all stakeholders have the opportunity to express their views."

This makes it clear that the meeting is solely to gather input, versus decide or design a campaign. Claire is both telegraphing to Bob that she wants his input as a key stakeholder while making it clear that she is the decision maker.

An ineffective statement of the meeting purpose, given Claire's role and objectives, would read something like:

- Review the upcoming marketing campaign
- Discuss the upcoming marketing campaign
- New marketing campaign

To varying degrees, each of the above statements ignores or blurs the distinction between the pig and the chickens. Each implies an ability to decide on aspects of the campaign, versus simply provide information or voice opinions about it. Even if the campaign truly is to be designed by committee, there will ultimately be one person accountable for it. There is a vast difference between a pig voluntarily making adjustments based on input she hears, versus being expected to make changes with which she does not agree. Claire has to make it clear, diplomatically but unambiguously, that while she is interested in input, the ultimate decision is hers.

It is remarkably easy, in all sorts of meeting contexts, for people to confuse pigs and chickens. Often, the problem is not that we don't know which is which; the problem is that the meeting purpose is unclear, which invariably leads to differing expectations, confusion or worse.

How many pigs and how many chickens?

The optimal number of attendees for an effective meeting depends entirely on the purpose of the meeting. In a presentation, this is a moot point. With most presentations, the more the merrier. But especially if the purpose of a meeting is to arrive at a decision, whom to invite is critical.

If the purpose of the meeting is to make a decision, invite all the pigs. Invite all the people who will be held accountable for the decision, who will have to implement the decision and who will be accountable for the results. You want as many pigs as possible in your meetings. They listen most acutely and they are most aware of what is at stake.

Venue: Temperature, Sound and Lighting

The physical environment matters. This is especially true with regard to meetings. Your meeting venue can either facilitate or inhibit your realizing the purpose of your meeting. Ignoring your meeting venue is like going skydiving without checking your parachute.

To lead a successful meeting, you must make sure that you attend to the three key aspects of the environment: Temperature, Sound and Lighting. If any of the three falls short, your meeting is at risk.

Temperature

Take the Goldilocks approach to temperature. Your meeting room can't be too warm or too cold. If your room is too warm, people will feel vaguely uncomfortable and will tend to fall asleep. The more meeting attendees, the more the people in attendance will heat up the room by virtue of their body heat. If you have a few people in a large room, this will not be a factor. If you have a lot of people in a small room, this definitely will be.

If your room is too cold, people's attention will shift from you and the meeting purpose to the room temperature. Too cold is admittedly slightly better than too hot, but why settle for either? Check your meeting room before your meeting. Have the temperature set slightly cooler than you might set it if you were in the room by yourself. This will allow for the body heat

generated by the attendees. When in doubt, go a few degrees cooler. It's better for people to don sweaters and jackets (within reason) than for them to want to peel off layers of clothes.

Be particularly sensitive to temperature in the spring and fall. In many a corporate office, temperature varies room to room year-round, but few things are worse than convening a meeting on a warm day in early spring only to discover that the heat in the building is still on and your room feels like a Bikram Yoga studio. Alternatively, you don't want to arrive at your meeting room on the first crisp day of fall only to discover that the air conditioner is still set for mid-July. Granted, there will be times when you will be unable to adjust the room temperature, but be aware of and prepared for it.

Sound

Acoustics matter. If people can't hear you or one another, your meeting will not be successful. In a small- or medium-sized conference room with a low number of attendees, this will not be an issue. But in virtually every corporate off-site meeting or presentation, sound is almost invariably a challenge.

Some rooms are better than others.

Carpets and curtains suck up sound. Typical hotel ballrooms are carpeted wall-to-wall and often have heavy drapery. This means that the people in the room, including you, are going to have to speak significantly louder than what seems normal in order to be heard. No speaker sounds as loud to the audience as he or she thinks.

The best rule of thumb is, *if you're not too loud, you're not loud enough.*

When in doubt, use a microphone. A wireless mike is best, so that you can move about at will. Make sure you test the mike carefully in advance, as wireless mikes can be notoriously fickle in terms of quality of sound and feedback. Try the mike in advance. Walk around the room speaking into it a bit, and get used to how you sound when mic'ed. Also, make sure to turn the mike off if you leave the room or want to have a private conversation. After a while, a functioning wireless mike is easy to forget. Be especially aware of this if, on a break, you head to the rest room.

Even when you wear a mike you must be cognizant of projecting your voice and speaking to people in the last row. Lowering your energy because you are wearing a mike will lessen the impact of your message. Think of the mike as a booster for projecting your voice, not as a substitute.

Taking Questions During Q&A

Have you ever attended a meeting at which the speaker took a question from the audience that you couldn't hear, and then addressed the question? Have you ever found yourself trying to infer what a question was based on a speaker's answer?

This happens all the time, in large and small meetings. It's frustrating for audience members who could not hear the question. Don't let this happen in your meeting.

The best way to ensure effective discussion between you as the meeting leader, and your audience, is to have two or three wireless hand-held mikes that people in your audience use to ask their questions. Ideally, someone raises his or her hand, is given or passed a mike, and asks a question. Everyone hears the question and stays engaged.

Passing microphones in this manner is tough to do for a couple of reasons. The first is the challenge of getting the mikes to people. Passing the mikes can be cumbersome, particularly in an auditorium or a room with classroom-style seating arrangements. It takes time, can slow down the proceedings, and can cause you to lose momentum.

The second reason is the audience. When you use hand-held mikes, you are virtually guaranteed that someone will raise his hand (it is almost invariably a "he") and proclaim, "I don't need a mike." Nine times out of ten, that will NOT be accurate. Very few people can accurately gauge how loudly they must speak in order to be heard.

If I am leading a session with Q & A, I will do one of two things. I will either simply restate the question so I am sure everyone has heard it (and that I have heard it correctly). I do this whether or not there are hand-held mikes in the room. Or, I will ask the audience, "Did everyone hear the question?" Invariably, someone says, "No." I then restate the question. Doing so helps involve everyone in the audience. It includes everyone in the dialogue. It communicates to audience members, "You're important enough to me for me to make sure you can hear what is going on", and, "I am not taking your attention for granted." In an effective meeting, the leader makes sure everyone can hear everything.

Lighting

Lighting is the toughest of the three challenges. Rooms with abundant natural light are best, but those are rare. Nothing beats meeting in a room with big windows that allow in abundant natural light, but even when such a room is available, meeting leaders often need to project slides onto a screen, so the room must be darkened periodically, which can make leaving the windows unshaded impractical. Nonetheless, if you can convene your meeting in a room with windows and light, you are starting ahead of the game. Never underestimate the impact that light, or lack thereof, has on people's moods.

Mood lighting may be great for a social event, but it is deadly for a meeting. Bad lighting makes it harder for people to see each other, interact, watch the speaker or pay attention.

During your pre-meeting room check, start by turning on all the lights and see if you can see everything in the room clearly from where you are standing. If you cannot, have additional lighting brought in. Floor lamps are best, but see what your other options might be. Obviously, the farther in advance you see a room and check the lighting, the more options you will have.

You should be able to see every corner of your room clearly enough to read a sign (with large enough letters). Everyone in your room should be able to see what you write on a flip chart (assuming you use one) clearly, again, assuming the lettering is large enough. Bright, non-fluorescent lighting is ideal. Brightly lit rooms are conducive to energy, enthusiasm and action. Dimly lit rooms are conducive to the opposite. Well-run hotels and conference centers know this, so in venues such as these you will likely be fine. Be especially aware of meeting rooms in cities best known for tourism, not corporate meetings. Paris may be a wonderful locale for a meeting; it is, after all, the most visited city in the world. It is, however, a challenging venue for a meeting.

For very big audiences, of a thousand or more, the lighting rule will not apply, as there will be a stage, multiple overhead screens, a darkened room and professional stage lighting. But in most cases, your ability to lead a successful meeting will be enhanced or inhibited as a function of the lighting in the room.

Preparation Complete

You've articulated a meeting purpose and an intended result. You have selected a venue and either checked, or made arrangements to check the sound, temperature and lighting. You've identified whom you want to attend your meeting.

You are beginning to think about when to hold your meeting, and whom to invite. You're ready for the next phase – **Invitation.**

Part 2

Invitation:
Putting the Rabbit in the Hat

You know what you want to accomplish. Now it's time to get others on board with your objective. That's what effective Invitation is about. It isn't just getting bodies to your meeting. Invitation is setting the stage. It is about teeing up what you want to get done.

First, the easy stuff

Schedule your meeting date and time as far in advance as you can. In a corporate setting, this may mean only a few days. But in other scenarios, such as when convening a meeting of a volunteer organization, Board of Trustees or Parents Association, more notice is always better. Send out as many "Save the Date" notices as you can without overdoing it. Don't be shy. You're competing for people's time and attention with a myriad of other things.

There is no such thing as the perfect date. Don't waste time and energy trying to find it. You should of course take your audience into consideration. Don't schedule a Parents meeting the Friday night before Spring Break. Don't schedule a sales meeting two days before the quarter close. (Sounds obvious but you'd be surprised….). Research as best you can, then establish a date knowing that it will not work for everyone. If there are specific individuals you absolutely must have in attendance, check their calendars. But don't drive yourself crazy trying to find a date that will work for everyone.

Plan to invite people any and every way you can: email, regular mail, Facebook Twitter and Text. Use carrier pigeon if possible. Don't worry about bombarding people. They are already bombarded. You are one of many competitors for their attention. People's preferences vary. Some prefer email, others, texts, still others, social media. Likely your attendees will include folks with each preference.

Logistics

Make sure you tell everyone everything he or she needs to know about getting to the meeting. The easier you make it for people, the more likely it is that they will attend. While this seems self-evident, you would be amazed how often key meeting details are overlooked.

Date and time are obvious. Here, for maximum effectiveness, give the day of the week and the date. "Monday, January 11" is preferable to "January 11." Don't just give the starting time, state the meeting duration. "7:30 pm – 9:30 pm" is preferable to "7:30 pm." Absent a scheduled ending time on the invitation, people will be left to guess or be obliged to ask you. Neither is what you want.

State your location so clearly that an out-of-town visitor could find it easily. How explicit you need to be will depend on your invitees. For a familiar group that has met before, "Executive Conference Room" may suffice. For a group that does not meet regularly, specify the location using an address and room number. "Houston Conference Center, 1010 Fannin Street, Room 2412" is better than "Houston Conference center, 1010 Fannin Street," which is, in turn, better than "Houston Conference Center."

In many places, parking is a concern. If you think parking will be an issue for your invitees (if it is for you, it will be for them), it is wise to include wording on the invitation to the effect of "Parking available in parking garage at 1020 Fannin," or, "Park in Visitors Lot on the 4th level." If people will attend using public transportation, you might want to include "One block from State Street Stop on Red Line" or "Greenville Plaza bus stop on Express and Local Center City Routes."

We all want to avoid hassle. When you don't provide clear details in your meeting invitation, you make people work to get to your meeting. The more work they have to do, they less likely it is that they will show up. To maximize attendance, maximize ease of attendance.

Purpose of the Meeting: The Key

You must state the purpose of the meeting clearly and directly in the invitation. This is essential. People need to know what you intend to accomplish and why you are requesting their time. This holds true even if you are the boss convening a meeting of your direct reports. Granted, if you are the boss, your folks will show up. But is that really how you want to lead?

In a very real sense, your meeting "begins" when you issue your invitation. You focus people's attention on an outcome or result. They start to interact mentally with that result as soon as they read your invitation. When they do, they start to move in the direction of your purpose. Even if a person's initial response is to resist your outcome, you have started the process through which whatever issue the invitee has can be resolved.

So why wouldn't someone clearly state the purpose of his or her meeting? Because he's afraid if he does, people won't come. Don't apologize for the meeting purpose and don't be disingenuous. Have you ever been invited to an event that you knew was a fundraiser but that was presented to you as something other than that? Which of the following invitations is the most honest?

- Come hear about all the great new things happening at Hoop de Doop School.
- Come hear about all the great new things happening at Hoop de Doop School and find out how you can support them
- Come hear about all the great new things happening at Hoop de Doop School and hear a presentation from Jane Jones, Director of Development, about the Annual Fund.

If the point of a meeting is to ask for money, make that known. There is no need to be blunt; "we're going to ask you for money" is probably not what you want to say. But no one who reads, "Hear a presentation from Jane Jones, Director of Development, about our Annual Fund" can possibly misinterpret that message. Just because something is subtle doesn't mean it isn't clear. Your invitations can be subtle or unsubtle, but your intent must be clear.

Pre-work

A meeting is most productive when the invitees arrive prepared. "Prepared" is defined as, "cognizant of and ready to achieve the purpose of the meeting." The more prepared people are for the meeting when they arrive, the faster the meeting will move towards achieving its intended purpose. For that reason, do everything you can do to ensure people come to the meeting armed with the information they need to discuss the agenda topics. Decide what that information is, and then organize and send it to attendees enough in advance so that they have sufficient time to read and digest it. The easier you make it for people to arrive prepared, the more likely it is that they will.

Of course before you can send pre-work, you have to finalize your meeting purpose and outcomes, both of which must be clearly stated in your request for people to review the pre-work materials. You can't expect people to spend time preparing for the meeting if they don't know why they should, and why they should depends on what the meeting is intended to produce.

People will be more likely to do the pre-work if you send an agenda along with the pre-work materials. This isn't essential, but it's highly desirable. For example, if an attendee knows that the purpose of the meeting is to establish the top three budget priorities for next year and allocate funds to each, and that the amount of time on the agenda for this topic is 90 minutes, she will realize she needs to come prepared to advocate for her preferences. She will know she needs to do the pre-work.

The huge advantage of pre-work is the message it sends to attendees. When you send well-prepared, thoughtful pre-work, with an agenda, you are telegraphing to attendees: "This meeting matters. We are prepared. We are going get something done together. We are not going to waste your time. We value your opinion. Please invest your time in getting ready; it will be worth it."

The most frequent objection to pre-work is, "No one will do it. People are too busy." The latter is true; people are busy. But if the meeting is important enough for people to attend, they will make time to come prepared. Even if they do not, you have still sent the message that the meeting will be productive.

People want to attend those kinds of meetings. Don't you?

Part 3

Agenda:
Putting the Rabbit in the Hat

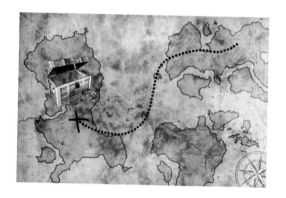

The heart of your meeting is your agenda. A well-done agenda doesn't guarantee you'll lead a great meeting, but your chances of leading a successful meeting without one are slim to none. Don't lead a meeting without an agenda.

A meeting agenda is like a roadmap. On a road trip, it's fine to detour so long as you make a conscious decision to do that. But unplanned detours take you off course and delay or prevent you from arriving at your destination.

It would be unwise to set sail from New York bound for England without a clear idea of the route you will take to get there. The same is true of a meeting. If you don't have a clear idea of how you are going to arrive at your objective, you almost certainly won't.

Agendas should be written. That's not always possible; sometimes meetings are called on short notice and there isn't time to print a formal agenda. But that's the exception. You should always prepare a written agenda, paying special attention to the timing of the topics you will cover. Even if you don't distribute the agenda to attendees in advance (which is preferable), you must at least plan the meeting carefully via a written agenda.

Meeting Purpose and Intended Results

The Meeting Purpose and Intended Results are your reference point and anchor. There should be a clear line of sight between the Meeting purpose and every item on the agenda. In fact, the purpose dictates the agenda.

The best agendas have the meeting purpose and intended result at the top of the page. That way everyone who reads the agenda knows what the meeting is about and what the meeting will accomplish. For example:

ABC Corporation
Executive Leadership Team Meeting
January 15 – 17, 2016

PURPOSE

- *Complete the 2015 company initiatives*
- *Articulate our 2016 corporate goals*
- *Align on what it will take to succeed given recent industry developments*
- *Build leadership capacity*

Here, the purpose and intended results are clear. At the end of a successful meeting, the attendees will have a written list of 2016 objectives. They will have completed, in some fashion, the current year's initiatives. They will have aligned on "what it will take to succeed. " They will have built leadership capacity. Please note, arguably only the 2016 corporate goals, and possibly aligning on what it will take to succeed, will be written. That's fine. There is a very easy way to verify that all the objectives have been met. More on that later in this chapter.

Detailed Agenda v. the Agenda for Distribution

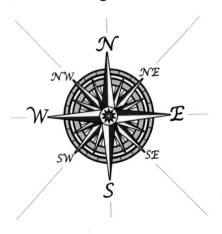

When I lead a meeting, I invariably start with a detailed version of the agenda. This detailed version has the purpose and intended results at the top. It then outlines the key sections of the meeting, with details of the points I want to make in each section. This serves two purposes. First, it helps me clarify my thinking regarding exactly what I want to cover, and often, what I want to say, in each section. Second, it helps me form a realistic idea of how long each section of the agenda will take. Moreover, if I will be using PowerPoint overheads during the meeting, this in effect "writes" the slides for me.

For example, this is part of a detailed agenda I wrote when I presented to the Chapter Presidents of US Lacrosse.

US LACROSSE NORTH NATIONAL MEETING
NORTH TEXAS CHAPTER PRESENTATION
SEPTEMBER 12, 2015
CHICAGO MARRIOTT DOWNTOWN

PURPOSE: *SHARE BEST PRACTICES ON HOW TO RUN A CHAPTER MEETING THAT IS CONSISTENT WITH THE VALUES OF US LACROSSE*

INTENDED RESULT: *ATTENDEES LEAVE WITH 1 – 3 TOOLS/TIPS THEY CAN USE IMMEDIATELY*

TIME		SPEAKER/ACTIVITIES/KEY POINTS
2:00	START	
2:00	WELCOME & INTRODUCTION	SARA
2:05	WHO IS THIS GUY AND WHY IS HE TALKING TO US?	DICK • NORTH TEXAS CHAPTER PRESIDENT • LACROSSE DAD WHO NEVER PLAYED • VOLUNTEERED FOR A BOARD ROLE • I AM FIGURING IT OUT AS I GO ALONG • PROFESSIONALLY I AM A MANAGEMENT CONSULTANT WHO WORKS WITH SENIOR TEAMS o I DESIGN AND FACILITATE LOTS OF MEETINGS o I HAVE LEARNED THROUGH TRIAL AND ERROR o HOPEFULLY SOME OF WHAT WE TALK ABOUT TODAY WILL BE USEFUL
2:15	MY OBJECTIVE FOR TODAY	DICK • FOR YOU TO LEAVE WITH AT LEAST ONE, AND PREFERABLY 2 – 3, TIPS, TOOLS OR TECHNIQUES YOU CAN USE RIGHT AWAY TO RUN YOUR CHAPTER MEETINGS MORE EFFECTIVELY AND MAKE YOUR LIFE EASIER
2:20	EXERCISE: YOUR OBJECTIVE FOR TODAY	DICK • GRAB A PENCIL AND PAPER. WITH REGARD TO YOUR CHAPTER MEETINGS, WHAT IS YOUR BIGGEST HEADACHE? • GET A PARTNER. DISCUSS YOUR ANSWER WITH YOUR PARTNER.

There are a couple of key points here. This is for my use only, not for distribution to attendees. If I were to distribute this agenda, I would do so without any of the bullets in green above (in this particular case, I did not hand out an agenda). I did, however, use PowerPoint overheads. One of the first overheads stated the Purpose and Intended Result and another showed the agenda without the bullets. Some of the bullets in green made it to the overheads; others did not. The key here is to think through the meeting. What do you want to say? More importantly, what do you want people to hear and remember? Your detailed agenda enables you to answer these questions.

A detailed agenda is especially important if you are leading a meeting at which others will speak, or co-leading a meeting, or even facilitating a meeting. You must clarify who will cover what meeting topic, when, before the meeting begins. In these cases, you should share your detailed agenda with everyone who will have a speaking role at your meeting. Abbreviated agendas are for people attending, not presenting. Everyone who has a speaking role at your meeting must be clear about and aligned with the meeting purpose and intended outcomes, as well as the path being taken to realize those.

Introductions and Rules of the Road: Optional but Key

There are two sections I consider including in every agenda. They are not always appropriate, but their potential impact on the success of the meeting is so important that I always consider them. The two sections are Introductions and Rules of The Road.

Introductions

For meetings of up to about fifteen people, when people don't already know each other, I like to do introductions. They're tricky, but they work, for several reasons. Anyone in a group of people, some of whom he or she does not know, will likely be some combination of curious, reserved or even shy. It's better to 'break the ice" and have people meet each other than to have people in a meeting wondering who the other people in the room  are. Brief introductions answer unspoken but very present questions, and allow everyone in the room to focus on the meeting and its intended outcome, not on the other people in the room.

Second, in some meetings, and especially in critical ones, a bedrock foundation of relationship and trust is essential. People need to know one another. Introductions enable people to connect, to find common areas of background or interest and to begin to build relationships.

Introductions are, however tricky. If you aren't careful, they will take more time than your agenda permits. We all love to talk about ourselves. Introductions must be structured carefully or people won't know what to say. Here is a short format for introductions that I use. I modify this format depending on whether I am in a corporate or non-corporate setting, but the outline remains essentially the same.

- Name
- Where you were born
- Where you live (non-corporate)
- How long with the organization and your current role (corporate)

- Your family, however you define it
- What you hope to achieve in this meeting (usually corporate but sometimes non-corporate)
- One non-work-related fact about you

There are many variations to this outline, depending on the specific meeting context.

If you decide to do introductions, write the introduction outline on a flip chart or overhead, so that people don't have to memorize what they are supposed to say or the order in which they are supposed to say it. Keep it short and simple.

Next, most importantly, introduce yourself according to your outline first. This serves several purposes. At least some of the people in the room will be wondering who you are. Your introduction tells them. Second, some people will think initially, "I don't know what to say." Your going first gives them time to craft a response, especially to the non-work-related fact question. Third, you should model being succinct in your response. You do want people to get to know each other. You don't want people to ramble on. If you are succinct, most people will be. Without fail, the longer the introductions proceed, the more people will talk. This is inevitable and except for the time factor, is actually a good thing. You will be pleasantly surprised at the tone in the room after introductions. You will see people relax and become more attentive.

Rules of the Road

At some meetings, Ground Rules, or, as I prefer to call them, *Rules of the Road* are a great idea. Rules of the Road establish parameters for how the meeting will be conducted, versus what the meeting will achieve. If you believe that Rules of the Road will expedite your realizing your meeting purpose, use them. If not, there is no need to. I like them when a group of people isn't used to working together, or when decisions need to be made and time is of the essence, or when I sense there are undercurrents of friction among some people attending. Use your instincts here; consider your purpose, attendees and how much time you have for the meeting.

Rules of the Road work only when people attending adopt them. One way to have that happen is to start with a blank sheet of paper, ask people to propose rules for the meeting, and have them do so. However, I never do this anymore. It takes too much time and people are often at a loss for what to suggest. Instead, I propose rules, explain them, ask people to propose additional rules, ask people if they are willing to adopt the rules, and then ask them to raise their hands to signify that they do.

Here are Rules of the Road I proposed for a senior team meeting of financial services executives:

- Talk straight. Say what you mean and mean what you say.
- What is said here stays here.
- No meetings after the meeting.
- When the group aligns, all debate stops.
- Be willing to put the moose on the table.
- Speak now or forever hold your peace.

"Moose on the table" refers to an issue that everyone in the room knows exists, but no one will bring up for whatever reason. People are invariably aware of these issues, and if an issue is present in the "unspoken" in a meeting and not addressed, pretense overwhelms candor and the meeting is doomed. "No meetings after the meeting" refers to the phenomenon wherein someone is silent in the meeting then complains afterwards about the meeting to someone else, rather than speaking up during the meeting itself. "Speak now or forever hold your peace" is my personal favorite. I can't abide meetings in which the purpose is to make a decision, people have opinions, don't voice them and then complain about, undermine or second-guess the decision after the fact. It leads to what my favorite client calls "Ground Hog Day," wherein you revisit the same decision over and over.

When you ask people to consider and then propose Rules of the Road, they begin to engage in the meeting – always a good thing. Also, you begin to hear clues about the concerns of people in the meeting. What does it tell you when someone proposes, "criticize ideas, not people"? How about "modulate your participation carefully – not too much or too little"? Or, "Be committed that this meeting make a real difference"? How about, "Put your cell phones and computers away"? Or, "Be comfortable with getting it roughly right"? All are Rules that participants have proposed for meetings I have conducted.

Timing – Art, not Science

One of the biggest challenges with agenda design is timing. How much time to allot to each topic on the agenda is an art, not a science. Simply make your best guess about how long to spend on each meeting topic, and stick as close to the timing as you can. You need to be flexible but not too flexible. On the one hand, you can never be sure which topic will generate the most participation, so if a particular topic runs over its allotted time, you have to be willing to go with the discussion. But if you aren't careful, the discussion will veer off on a tangent and you will not realize the meeting objective. Moreover, more time allotted to topic A, in a meeting with a fixed ending time, means less time allotted to Topic B. It's a zero-sum game, which is why adhering to an agenda can be so tricky. We'll talk about this topic further in our next section – **Delivery.**

Now the Rabbit's (Finally) in the Hat.

You have articulated your meeting purpose and intended results, selected a meeting venue, invited your attendees, written an agenda, and distributed the agenda and meeting pre-work to attendees. You're finally ready to convene your meeting.

On to **Delivery.**

Part 4

Delivery:
Pulling the Rabbit Out of the Hat

Whether a meeting is the first you have ever led or the thousandth, how you lead it will either enhance or undercut your chances of success. There are basic steps you can take to maximize the odds in your favor. Think of these steps as what's required to maintain the integrity of the meeting. In this case, integrity simply means, whole, complete, and missing no constituent part. "Integrity" here connotes no sense of right/wrong or good/bad. It is used in the sense of missing or not missing.

Start on Time

 Well-run meetings start on time. Some people hate to hear that, but it's true. If your meeting is scheduled to start at 11:00 am, close the door to the meeting room at 11:00 and start. Doing so serves a number of purposes. It signifies that you value people's time – the attendees' and yours. It conveys a sense of professionalism. It is a statement that you mean business and intend that the meeting succeed. Also, if a meeting is held regularly, such as a monthly staff meeting, people will quickly learn whether you are serious about your start time and plan accordingly.

I have worked in Fortune 50 corporations in which the corporate culture treats the start time of a meeting as a rough estimate. People show up for a meeting scheduled at 9:00 am around 9:00 or so, chat for a while and then start the meeting between 9:10 and 9:15. In this company, meetings are notorious for running late, and administrative assistants are constantly juggling schedules. People resign themselves to inefficiency and lack of rigor. In this same corporation, people are surprised when critical product, marketing or customer deadlines are missed.

But even in this company there are a few leaders who buck the trend. Their meetings start on time and people know that. I have seen people leave a meeting in progress to go to a meeting led by one of these executives because they know it will start on time. These leaders tend to be "rising stars" or "high potentials."

Delaying announcement

At times there may be reasons not to start exactly on time. As the meeting leader, you may want to give people a few extra minutes to arrive, sit down, take out their materials or get settled. This is often the case if you are leading a meeting for a volunteer organization. You may think to yourself, "I think I'll just wait and start in five or ten minutes to give people a chance to get here."

The dilemma here is that some people did arrive on time, and you are in effect saying to them, "I know you expended the effort to get here on time, but your effort doesn't matter enough to me to start on time. " Moreover, you don't want to send a message to them of "my meetings don't really start on time, so next time you can arrive late." The solution here is to make a delaying announcement. At the meeting start time, call the meeting to order and say something like,

"Good morning. Welcome. It's 7:00pm. We are scheduled to start now, and a few people are still arriving due to [the weather, parking, a meeting in the other building that ran late, etc.]. *We going to give people a few more minutes to arrive and get settled, and we'll be starting the meeting at 7:05, in five minutes. Please make yourselves comfortable, as we'll start shortly. Thank you for your patience."*

Ten minutes should be the maximum you ever postpone your start. Your meeting should end on time, and depending on how long your meeting is, ten minutes may cut into your agenda significantly. It is also the longest delay you should impose on the people who arrived promptly; five minutes is far better. And needless to say, you must start exactly when you say you will without fail, or you have shot your own credibility.

There are two ways, then, to preserve the integrity of your meeting at the outset. You can

• Start on time, or

• Announce a delay with a new start time, and start exactly at the new time.

Attendance

Whenever feasible, account for the people expected to attend the meeting. In large, formal presentations this does not apply, but in many meetings, such as staff or Board meetings, it does.

For example, if I as Chairman call a Board Meeting, and the Board consists of eight people including me, I will have confirmed the attendance of everyone in advance, typically via calendar software such as Outlook Meeting Invitation or iCal. Let's say that of the seven Board members excluding myself, six have confirmed their attendance, and one has declined; she is out of town on business. Everyone else has confirmed. The day of the meeting I get a message from one Board member saying he may be 15 – 20 minutes late due to a last minute business appointment. Fifteen minutes before the meeting, scheduled for 7:00, I get a text from another member saying he is stuck in traffic and may be ten minutes late.

At 7:00 I convene the meeting. After thanking everyone for coming, I say, *"Beth is out of town and wasn't scheduled to be here. Anthony had a last-minute conference call and will be here between 7:15 and 7:20. Jeff is on his way, stuck in traffic on 635. He should be here in 15 minutes."*

Every Board member has now been accounted for. No one spends the first few minutes of the meeting wondering where other Board members are. The integrity of the meeting is preserved.

If you don't account for people expected to be present, other attendees' attention will inevitably be diverted from the meeting and its purpose to speculating as to where those absent are, why they are absent, whether this meeting was really important, etc. None of that is good.

What happens if someone is a "No Show?" If that happens, say so clearly but without indictment. If an attendee is expected to show and doesn't, it may be for any number of valid reasons. In the example above, had someone No Showed, I might have said, *"Pat isn't here. He's confirmed and I don't know why he's not here."* People will wonder momentarily what happened to Pat, but they will quickly move on if you do. Again, saying precisely what's so preserves the integrity of the meeting.

Distribute the agenda

It's a good idea to give everyone a copy of the agenda, or to display the agenda on an overhead slide. This is true even if you have sent the agenda to people in advance. It helps people follow the flow of the meeting. This also recommits you, as the leader, to adhering to your agenda and timeline. Via the agenda, everyone knows your intent and your timeline. They become partners with you in achieving the purpose of the meeting.

Purpose and Intended Results

After attendance, focus immediately on the purpose and intended results of the meeting. Review and re-read them. After you do, pause, look around the room, and make sure everyone is clear about them. Next, refer to the agenda, briefly review the major sections of the agenda, and note the ending time of the meeting for everyone.

Occasionally, you may want to ask either if anyone has any questions about the purpose of the meeting, or wishes to add anything to the agenda. People rarely do, but it may be wise to ask. On the rare occasions that they do, even though you may need to devote time at the beginning of the meeting to discussing either the purpose, intended results or agenda, everyone benefits from surfacing any potential questions, conflict or misunderstanding at the beginning of the meeting. Moreover, once you validate your purpose and agenda with the attendees, you have their implicit endorsement. You can proceed with velocity.

Delivery: Memorize your first three sentences

The opening of any meeting or presentation is the hardest part. All of us, regardless of our level of experience, are usually at least a bit uncertain and/or awkward when we first stand in front of a group or open a meeting. As a result, our attention is on ourselves, not on the people in our meeting. If we need to think about what we want to say, our focus is off the attendees and the purpose of the meeting.

The solution to this dilemma lies in your preparation for the meeting. Before the meeting, write down your first three sentences – the first three sentences you will say when you open the meeting. Write them out at least a day or two in advance. Choose every word carefully. After your first draft, go off and do something else, then come back to your first three sentences a few hours (or more) later. Look at the

sentences again. Are they exactly right? Once they are, memorize them. Say them until you don't need to think about them. If time permits, say them into the mirror so that the person in the mirror hears and understands them.

When you open your meeting, you can look at your audience, the attendees, and focus your attention on them, versus on what you are going to say. This is invaluable. When you focus on your audience, they focus on you and on what you have to say. Yes, you may want to ad lib your opening, or change what you start with. You can always do that on the spot, in the moment. But it is far better to be armed with your opening and not use it, than to need it and not have it prepared. I have even on occasion built gaffes into my opening three sentences, on purpose, if I think that will help me achieve my purpose.

Memorizing your first three sentences increases your chances of establishing credibility and approachability. Every speaker starts out stronger on one and needs to build the other. Someone may be immediately credible but not particularly easy to relate to. For her, memorizing her first three sentences enables her to focus on the audience and put her attention on connecting with the people to whom she is speaking. Someone else may exude warmth but need to establish a sense of "I know what I am talking about." For him, memorizing his first three sentences enables him to present himself as knowledgeable and competent. Either way, the meeting leader enhances his or her chances of success.

The Podium is Not Your Friend

Avoid speaking from behind a podium at all costs. It may be inevitable; in a hotel ballroom with 1500 – 200 people, you may be obliged to. But unless there is absolutely no way you can avoid the podium, stay away from it. It establishes a barrier between you and your audience. It is conducive to a stiff, overly formal delivery. It inhibits your gesturing with your hands. Unless you are reading a speech (never a great idea, but occasionally necessary) and need the podium to hide your script, get out from behind it as soon as possible.

The two best antidotes to a podium are a wireless mike and overheads. With a wireless mike, you can get out from behind the podium and walk around the stage or among the members of your audience. Simply doing that will enhance the interpersonal connection between you and your audience. Overheads direct people's attention to the screen and the material on it. You can refer to the overheads, use them as your notes and therefore not need the podium for any reason.

Other Tips for Delivery

Here are a couple of other suggestions for delivering your meeting powerfully. They are applicable in some situations, not in others.

Keep your hands above your belt line. If you will be leading your meeting while standing, and are concerned about what to do with your hands, focus only on keeping them above your belt line. If you do, your hands will take care of themselves. Keep your hands visible; don't put them in your pockets, fold your arms, or clasp them behind your back. Your hands will move in concert with what you say if you let them.

Talk to the last row. We all sound louder to ourselves when we talk than we actually are in reality. Nothing is worse than being in a meeting unable to hear the speaker. Particularly at the beginning of your meeting, focus your attention on the people farthest away from you. Speak to them. After you begin, ask them if they can hear you. Once they can, ask them to please raise their hands if at any time they cannot hear you or whoever is speaking.

A common mistake speakers make is to think that if they are mic'ed, they don't need to project. Just because you are talking into a mike doesn't mean you don't need to consciously intend that everyone hear you. You will almost certainly sound too loud to your own ears. Don't let that deter you. In fact, to repeat what I said earlier, if you're not "too loud," you're not loud enough.

Stick to Your Timeline (or say you're changing it)

Unless you are delivering a presentation with no opportunity for audience interaction, sticking to your agenda timeline is one of the key challenges of leading a successful meeting. As we said in *Agenda,* this is an art, not a science.

Here is where the meeting purpose becomes invaluable. As the meeting leader, be hyper-aware of your meeting purpose. If you sense that the discussion is in line with the purpose and moving you towards your objective, albeit perhaps circuitously or indirectly, let the discussion proceed. If you sense otherwise, stop the discussion, acknowledge the issue, and capture it on a list of "Parking Lot" items – topics to be dealt with separately after the meeting. The path to achieving your meeting purpose very often is not a "straight line;" discussions rarely unfold as we envision. As long as the discussion is directionally correct, you're fine. As meeting leader (remember, you're the pig here), you are the one to determine whether it is.

Let's say you've allotted fifteen minutes to a particular topic, and that you've already spent 13 – 14 minutes on it. The discussion is lively, people are engaged, and your sense is that the group is moving in the direction of achieving the meeting purpose. At an appropriate time, usually when there is a pause between speakers, you as the meeting leader can say, *"we are at the amount of time on the agenda for this topic, but let's continue this discussion for another ten minutes before we move on."*

This preserves the integrity of the meeting agenda. You're changing the agenda, but you're doing so openly. This is distinct from allowing the discussion to proceed and not acknowledging it. It is fine to make changes; it's even fine to completely blow up your agenda during the meeting. They key is to do it consciously, volitionally and pro-actively. It's your meeting. You have a purpose to achieve, and if there is a better way to do that, or if you need to change course during the meeting, you can and should.

What you should not do is pretend that you're sticking to your agenda when everyone can see that you're not. When time runs over on an agenda item and you don't say so, it calls into question everything from the validity of the agenda, to the purpose of the meeting, to your control of the meeting.

Don't Get Hijacked – Covertly or Overtly

At times a discussion will veer off topic. This can happen for a variety of reasons. In one sense this is harmless; most of us don't realize when we embark on a conversational tangent. We have a normal, human tendency to think that because something is interesting to us, it is interesting for everyone. The problem is, in a meeting, time is a finite resource, and discussions that are off topic move the meeting away from realizing its purpose. I call this being hijacked covertly.

As meeting leader, if you realize a discussion has moved away from its intended focus, you must diplomatically reframe the discussion in a way that does not invalidate the person speaking. This isn't always easy. First, you have to wait for the speaker to pause. Usually this isn't a problem, but it can be. Next, you have to make sure the speaker knows that you appreciate his or her point of view and contribution to the meeting. (Forget whether you think the comments actually contribute; that's beside the point.) Next, you should reference the purpose of the meeting as your rationale for redirecting the dialogue. You can say something like, *"We really appreciate the great points your making about the need for better officiating at the youth games. I've noted your points and would like to discuss them with you further off line. Just to remind ourselves, the purpose of our meeting is to establish the dates for the fall and spring tournaments, and we were discussing whether a March or April date presents fewer conflicts for Spring. I think I am hearing that people prefer April. Is that accurate?"*

This way, you as meeting leader steer the meeting back on course without invalidating the person taking it off course. You must steer clear of two pitfalls. The first occurs if, in the interest of being polite, or because you're too timid, you don't speak up, the meeting veers off topic and the purpose isn't realized. As a result, people leave the meeting irritated and feel their time has been wasted. The other pitfall, less common but no less hazardous, is that you somehow make the person off on the tangent feel foolish or defensive. You won't mean to, but I have found that the more unaware a speaker off on a tangent is of his digression, the more likely he is to become offended when you call his digression to his attention. Do so gently. Other attendees are invariably aware that the discussion has veered off course and will appreciate your refocusing it.

Hijacked Overtly

Although it is rare that you as the meeting leader will be openly challenged by an attendee who wants to take the meeting in an entirely different direction or promote his or her agenda, it does happen. Having worked with leaders for decades, I am convinced that if you're prepared for and therefore unafraid of this happening to you, it probably won't. To the extent you're unprepared for it or worried it could happen, it probably will. It has happened to me.

Two years ago, as the newly installed President of the Board of a regional chapter of US Lacrosse, I convened my first public meeting. The purpose of the regional chapter is to support the sport of lacrosse in our region. The job of the Board it to make that happen. The purpose of the meeting was to solicit input from people in the region as what they wanted the Board to do. We invited everyone in the region, emailing our entire mailing list. Here is the detailed agenda I prepared.

North Texas Chapter US Lacrosse
Constituent Support Budget Process Meeting

SMU Cox School Of Business
Crum Auditorium
August 14, 2014

Purpose

- Solicit North Texas Lacrosse Program views on how the North Texas Chapter can support the growth of lacrosse in North Texas

- Inform the North Texas Chapter Board as it prepares its 2014-15 budget submission to US Lacrosse Baltimore

Thursday, Aug 14, 2014

Time		Activities / Key Points
7:00	Start	
7:00	Welcome & Introductions	Dick • North Texas Chapter Board members • US Lacrosse Staff members
7:10	Format for the evening	Dick • Each member program will be given 5 minutes to present its suggestions and requests • After each presentation, there will be up to 5 minutes for questions from Board members • Ten minutes maximum per program • If all programs in attendance have spoken before 9:00 PM there will be an open session Q&A • Evening will end promptly at 9:00 PM
7:20	Determine how many programs are represented and wish to speak	Dick • "If you are here tonight representing a North Texas Program and would like to have the floor this evening, please stand up so that we can gauge whether our proposed timing will work." • Board members count number of people who wish to present • Adjust timing of evening if necessary
7:25	Individual Member Program Presentations	Dick captures responses on flip charts • Assumes 8 – 10 member program presentations
8:45	Synthesis and Summary	Dick
8:55	Concluding Remarks	Dick
9:00	Adjourn	

The meeting was held in an auditorium. About 125 people were present. I opened the meeting, introduced myself, and stated the purpose of the meeting. Almost immediately, a gentleman, seated in about the sixth row, raised his hand and asked me if everyone else on the Board was from my town. The tone of the question wasn't friendly, but that was fine. The other Board members were there, they were from around the region and I was planning on them introducing themselves. They did.

I then presented the format for the meeting. He again interrupted, and asked a question about Board Finances unrelated to the purpose of the meeting. I responded. He then asked question on a different topic. At this point I realized I was in trouble. I now knew that if I didn't neutralize him, in the least confrontational way possible, the meeting I was planning to have wasn't going to happen. There would be no way to achieve the purpose. I didn't know why he wasn't happy, but the reasons didn't matter at that point.

How to Respond

I started by asking, *"Do you want to be here?"* My objective here was to remind him that it was his choice to attend the meeting. No one was forcing him to be there. When challenged in a meeting you are leading, this is important. If the person says, "no," you can thank them for coming. They leave, and your problem is solved. If the person says, "yes," you have now reestablished that it is his choice to be there. No one is forcing him. In this case, the gentleman said, "yes."

Once someone has confirmed that he or she does in fact want to be in your meeting, refer back to the purpose of the meeting. Your purpose tells everyone, "This is the meeting we are having here, now." There are many meetings we could be having. But *this* is the one that we are having." In this instance, as politely as I could, I said that this was the meeting we would be having that evening, that I was happy to talk to him off line about his concerns, and that we would be moving forward.

If something like this happens to you, you must have the courage of your convictions and meet the challenge head on. That means that while I never want to be unnecessarily adversarial, as leader of the meeting; I am the "pig." I'm accountable. In this case, this was the Chapter's meeting. We rented the room, we invited people, we drafted the agenda. It's our meeting. If someone is attempting to hijack your meeting to promote his own agenda, you should encourage him to convene his own meeting, where he can promote his agenda. But in your meeting, you will follow your agenda, not his.

Here the story ends with the gentleman in question asking if he could say one more thing. I told him that yes, he could, and that this would be his last comment in the meeting, as there were others present from whom we needed to hear. He said something. I listened, thank him and moved back to the agenda. He stayed for another half-hour or so and then left.

Capture Decisions and Action Items

Designate someone, in advance whenever possible, as scribe, whose job is to take meeting notes. This task is less onerous than it sounds, since the only notes that should be captured are decisions made and action items to which those present commit.

When there is a decision, make sure that the decision is worded the way you, as the meeting leader, want it worded. Have the scribe read the decision back, so that you and everyone present can agree on the content of the decision. After the meeting, when meeting notes are distributed, you will want to make sure that those notes represent the meeting accurately. That requires you to ensure that the notes taken during the meeting are correct. Taking time to ensure that they are can save you time and headaches later.

Mid-meeting Process Check

At times you may want to pause midway through your meeting, refer to your meeting purpose, and ask the group whether people feel the meeting is on track or whether you should course correct. For example, if you aren't sure if people are engaged, you may want to stop and check in with people. This can only benefit you. If the meeting is on track to achieve its purpose, people will say so. You will be reassured, and their ownership of the meeting increases. If the meeting is not on track, people will say so, you find out sooner rather than later, and you can course correct together with your attendees. Again, this can only benefit you.

Usually it is apparent when a meeting is on track, so mid-meeting process checks tend to be remedial, but not always. If your instincts tells you to check in with people during the meeting, you should.

Concluding the Meeting

The best meetings end strongly. As the meeting draws to a close, revisit the purpose and intended results. It should by now be apparent that the meeting has achieved its purpose. When everyone in attendance acknowledges that, it reinforces each person's sense of his or her time having been well spent. If the purpose in whole or in part has not been realized, saying so maintains the integrity of the meeting and, not incidentally, your credibility as the meeting leader. Sometimes even the best-planned meetings aren't successful. When that is the case, everyone knows. Should that happen, it is best that you as the meeting leader be the one to point it out.

End on time

Don't have your meeting exceed its scheduled time. Make sure everyone is aware that you are aware of the scheduled ending time. If it looks as though your meeting could run a few minutes late, before the set ending time, you might say, *"We're scheduled to end at 10:30. I'm going to ask that we go 10 minutes late and end at 10:40. Please stay if you can, but if you can't, no problem. Thank you for being here."*

This serves several purposes. It lets everyone know that you are aware of your scheduled ending time and take it seriously. It communicates your respect for people's time. It preserves the integrity of the meeting; just as you start when you promised, you end when you promised. It gives people a choice as to whether they stay late, so that the people that do, have chosen to do so. Not giving people that choice puts them in the uncomfortable position of either having to interrupt to excuse themselves from the meeting, or of staying later than they had planned with the likely result that they resent the incursion on their time.

Say What's Next

After underscoring that the meeting purpose has been realized, let people know next steps as appropriate. For example, if a purpose of the meeting was to identify key initiatives for next year, you could say, "we will be distributing the Initiatives List next week. Action plans will be due by the end of the month. The first quarterly progress review will be in April." The point here is to leave people with a sense of forward momen-

tum - progress towards the objectives for which the meeting was convened. If notes of the meeting are being distributed to attendees, make sure people know who will distribute meeting notes, and by when.

Meeting Evaluation

When feasible, it is very helpful to you as the meeting leader, to solicit honest feedback about the meeting and your leadership of it. The best way is via anonymous, written feedback immediately following the meeting. I like to do this via a written form for people to complete, a sample of which is on the following page. They key here is to keep it short (never more than one page) and specific.

ABC Organization
XYZ Meeting – Date
Evaluation

	Not at all (1)	Very little (2)	Some-what (3)	Mostly (4)	Yes (5)
I knew the purpose of the meeting and why I was invited to attend.					
The meeting objectives were clear.					
The meeting was well organized and well run.					
The facilitator (Dick) did a good job					
The meeting objectives were met.					
This meeting was a good use of my and my colleagues' time.					

What I liked most about this meeting was _____

_____

_____

This meeting could have been improved by _____

_____

_____

Comments _____

_____

_____

Distribute the evaluation sheets at the end of the meeting. Have people complete them and leave them face down in a pile for you. Most people appreciate being asked for their opinion, and you will learn a lot.

Thank People for Attending and Specifically Adjourn

Finally the second-to-last thing you should say is, *"Thank you for attending. And for your time."* The last thing you should say is, *"Meeting Adjourned."* This lets people know that it is time to leave. It bookends the meeting nicely and gives people a sense of completion. Although I can't prove it, I believe it adds credibility to the meeting and imparts a sense of satisfaction to participants of having accomplished something.

You meeting has now been delivered. Keep your momentum going with effective **Follow Up.**

Part 5

Follow Up

In many ways, Follow Up is the hardest step of all. Effective follow up often means the difference between a meeting that is moderately successful versus one that has a major impact. People can leave a meeting with different ideas of what was decided and what occurred. Over time, individual recollections usually diverge. If the results of a meeting are not captured promptly and accurately in writing, all the work that went into the meeting can be lost. Conversely, well-done meeting notes help build a track record of progress and accomplishment.

Always Capture your Meeting Results

Effective Follow Up is always in writing. As soon as possible after a meeting, have the scribe – the note taker – send you his or her notes from the meeting. Review the notes with the purpose of the meeting in mind. Based on the notes, is it clear that the meeting purpose was realized? In many ways, what is said about the meeting after it has occurred is as if not more important than what actually happened in the meeting. Read the meeting notes carefully, and don't hesitate to amend the scribe's wording to add clarity and specificity.

Emphasize what was decided and accomplished. Check for

- What?
- Who?
- When?

"What" refers to the specifics of what was decided. Make sure it is clear what is going to happen that would otherwise not have happened had the meeting not occurred. Be as specific as you can. *"The Spring Tournament was scheduled"* is not as effective as *"The Spring Tournament will be held April 2-3 at Highlander Stadium."* *"Sales people will submit their initial requests to Marketing"* is not as effective as *"Sales people will submit their initial request to Kyle Chester in Marketing by June 1."*

"Who" refers to the person accountable for a specific action. Don't skip this step. Remember pigs and chickens; the pig is accountable, the chicken is involved. *"Each team will pay a tournament fee of $50 to participate"* is not nearly as effective as *"A team tournament fee of $50 will be payable to HJK Lacrosse at time of registration. Hank Kaye will acknowledge receipt of fees and compile the tournament roster."* For each action item in your notes, ask yourself, *"Who is accountable for making this happen?"* If you don't know, make a note to yourself to either find out or designate someone.

"When" is always a specific date and time. It is fine to say, *"Nominations are due to Jack Smith as soon as possible,"* so long as you add *"and will close Friday, May 5th."* Never assume that people reading the notes of the meeting will share the same sense of timing or urgency. In the absence of specific dates and times, people can justifiably feel free to attend to an action item whenever convenient. If you aspire to action, make sure your meeting notes reflect what you want to happen as specifically as possible.

Once you are satisfied with the notes from the meeting, email the notes to meeting attendees and to those invited to the meeting who were absent. Your note should include:

- Purpose and Intended Results
- Date and Time
- Attendees
- Actions taken and/or decisions made
- Follow up actions as appropriate
- Next meeting date, as applicable

Keep it brief

Meeting Notes should be brief and to the point. They should not include who said what, how long a topic was discussed, or the differing points of view represented in the meeting. Meeting Notes produce closure and, more importantly, action. They are not about the process. They are solely about the outcome.

Part 6

In Conclusion

As a leader, your meetings represent you. They reflect your ability to think, plan, articulate and execute. They are one of many expressions of your facility with people and process. There is no such thing as a great leader who runs mediocre meetings. World-class chefs don't serve their meals in Styrofoam containers.

When you take the time to plan and execute an effective meeting, you communicate your respect and regard for people's time and attention. You demonstrate that you use resources wisely and for maximum impact. You have no need to talk about efficiency and velocity; you personify efficiency and velocity.

Leading effective meetings isn't complicated. It simplify requires a willingness to value other people's time as you do your own and to invest time in treating people's presence and attention as a gift, not as an entitlement. Anyone can lead great meetings.

The key question is what you, the leader, are trying to achieve. The simpler the objective, the less preparation time required. It is one thing to plan the annual meeting, quite another to clarify the strategy for the coming year, yet another to articulate and align on the corporate culture needed to effect the strategy. Sometimes planning time is measured in hours, other times in days, and still other times in weeks.

Regardless of the objective, the principles are the same. Follow the roadmap outlined in the previous pages and let me know if you have any questions.

You can do this. You will. After you do, let me know how it went. I'd love to hear.

All the best,

Dick Massimilian
dmassimilian@meritaspartners.com

Acknowledgements

Sometimes you don't know what you know until someone asks you to write it down. Such was the case here. Thank you to Sara Noon and Steve Kirr of US Lacrosse for the opportunity to work with a great group of volunteers. Their encouragement started the process that culminated in this book. Thank you to Tommy Nusz, Taylor Reid and the team at Oasis Petroleum for building the best corporate environment I have encountered in more than twenty-five years as a management consultant and for the opportunity to learn many of the lessons presented herein. Finally, thank you to my brother, Robert, whose advice and counsel has been invaluable and without whom this book would never have made it to print.